WARRIOR OF LIGHT
The Life of Nicholas Roerich

*Artist,
Himalayan Explorer
and Author*

COLLEEN MESSINA

SUMMIT UNIVERSITY ⚜ PRESS®

WARRIOR OF LIGHT
The Life of Nicholas Roerich
Artist, Himalayan Explorer and Author
by Colleen Messina

Cover: *Moses the Leader*, a painting by Nicholas Roerich.
Bolling Collection, Naples, Florida. Used by permission.

Photographs courtesy of the Nicholas Roerich Museum.

Library of Congress Control Number: 2002102789
ISBN: 0-922729-79-4
66 p. : ill.
SUMMIT UNIVERSITY ☙ PRESS®

For my parents,

Dr. Harvey and Violet Bird,

who surrounded me with culture

and introduced me to my master,

Nicholas Roerich

CONTENTS

CHAPTER I

"One Who Overcomes, Rich in Glory"

"Rigden Djapo's eyes never close. In his magic mirror, he sees everything that happens on earth. His powerful light can destroy all darkness."

The storyteller's piercing blue eyes blazed in his tanned, bearded face. His melodious voice went on, "Rigden Djapo is the ruler of Shamballa, a secret place in a hidden Himalayan valley that is the link between heaven and earth. His throne is made of blue wings surrounded by flowers."

In the cozy living room in St. Petersburg, Russia, the Roerich family and their friends sat spellbound. Soft lamplight surrounded the cluster of comfortable chairs. The occasional muffled beat of horses' hooves floated up from the snowy street below. The rest of the city was preparing for bed, but no one in the room was interested in sleep.

"It is said that great darkness will some day

1

come upon the earth. There will be wars, kingdoms will be destroyed and underground fires will shake the earth.

"And one great day," concluded the storyteller, leaning forward in his chair, "Rigden Djapo will assemble his army and lead the warriors of light in a victorious fight against evil. Then the great era of Shamballa will begin. Peace and beauty and truth will reign over all the earth."

The room fell silent except for the crackle of flames in the fireplace, as the friends sat lost in thought about the promised era of Shamballa. No one had noticed the tired, fair-haired little boy hiding behind an armchair. Electrified by the story, he was thinking over and over, "That's me! I am a warrior of light. I am a warrior of light!"

As the group began to stir, his mother found him in his hiding place. "Nicholas," she chided, "you are supposed to be in bed!"

"I know, Mama, but I wanted to hear the story!" Gently, his mother sent him off to dream fantastic dreams.

Nicholas Konstantin Roerich was born on October 9, 1874, in St. Petersburg. From the beginning, he had a lot to live up to. "Nicholas" means "one who overcomes" and "Roerich" means "rich in glory."

When Nicholas grew up, he became a twentieth-century Renaissance man. He had at least seven careers: artist, writer, philosopher, explorer, educator, archaeologist and international leader for peace. He was a glorious overcomer in many ways.

The Roerichs' home was on the bank of the Neva River in St. Petersburg. Nicholas's father, Konstantin, was a serious-looking man with a flowing beard. Trained as a lawyer, he was a successful notary who helped his clients with wills and other legal matters. His office was on the first floor of their home. Nicholas's mother, Maria, was a sturdy woman with wide-set eyes. She kept house for her family on the second floor. Nicholas had an older sister, Lidia, and two younger brothers, Boris and Vladimir.

Guests often visited the Roerichs in the evening. The Roerichs knew many famous and interesting people, and lively discussions were the entertainment. Some of the guests talked about

ROERICH FAMILY PORTRAIT, EARLY 1880S.
LEFT TO RIGHT: MARIA, BORIS, LIDIA, KONSTANTIN AND NICHOLAS

politics, science or art. Others told stories about their exotic journeys across Asia and what they had learned on their travels. Whenever Oriental topics came up, Nicholas was all ears. Caravans! Eastern adventures! What could be more fascinating?

Even with these exotic tales to think about, Nicholas still had to go to school. But he didn't start at age five or six. Like most upper-middle-class Russian children at that time, Nicholas was taught at home by private tutors until age nine. Then he took the entrance exams for a rigorous private school headed by a professor named Karl von May. When Nicholas easily passed the exams, the professor exclaimed, "Here we have a future professor!"

Nicholas proudly became a "May bug," as Professor von May's students were called. Each day, he ate an early breakfast and walked the short distance to school in the clear morning light. The professor would be waiting at the top of the inside staircase to greet each student. He was a short, bearded man with gold-rimmed spectacles. He always wore a long black coat with a bright red and yellow handkerchief poking out of the pocket.

"Good morning, Nicholas," Professor von May would say. "Welcome to school!" And he would shake Nicholas's hand vigorously.

"Good morning, Professor," Nicholas would reply. He learned to hold on tight and return the handshake with a good strong grip. Perhaps this helped Nicholas later when he visited so many foreign countries and met so many important people.

Nicholas excelled in all subjects, but his favorite was geography. He especially loved to draw and color the large maps assigned by Professor von

May, who was his favorite teacher. The maps reminded Nicholas of the faraway places his parents' guests talked about.

Nicholas also loved his professor's three-dimensional geography assignments: sculpting mountain ranges out of plasticine, which is like clay. One day, as he sat at a table finishing a model of the Alps, he had an especially dreamy look in his eyes. The soft, sweet smell of spring was blowing in through the open window.

"Nicholas, you have plasticine on your nose! What are you daydreaming about?" asked one of his friends.

Nicholas wiped off his nose, pushed up his glasses and whispered, "Isvara."

CHAPTER 2

Holidays at Isvara

Nicholas liked St. Petersburg, but his favorite place in all the world was the family's 3,000-acre estate, Isvara. There they spent summers and winter holidays. Later Nicholas would say, "Everything special, everything pleasant and memorable is connected with the summer months at Isvara."

The original owner of the estate had named it after returning from a trip to India. "Isvara" is a Sanskrit word. One of its meanings is "sacred dwelling" or "ashram."

Isvara was about fifty-five miles from St. Petersburg. It was a boy's paradise, a place for adventures like the ones in Nicholas's storybooks. Its magic influenced Nicholas for the rest of his life.

The two-story manor house, built of white stone, was surrounded by a large park. Close by was

7

a lake. The fresh pines in the huge forest nearby smelled wonderful. Nicholas loved to hike over the lush hills and dip his feet into the cold, trickling streams. What a relief it was, after the stale city smells of St. Petersburg, to fill his lungs with the delicious air!

Nicholas often lay on the grass and gazed at the vast northern skies. He imagined all kinds of pictures in the ever-changing clouds. Over there was a horse and rider, there a hero with a turban!

Other things at Isvara inspired his imagination. On a wall in the manor house hung a magnificent painting of a snow-capped mountain in the Himalayas named Kanchenjunga. The scene was bathed in the fiery glow of sunset. "Some day I will visit a mountain like that, and I will have adventures, too," thought Nicholas. He imagined himself on a shaggy horse or a sturdy yak trudging up and down snowy slopes. Many years later, Nicholas did his own painting of Kanchenjunga. It became very famous.

Summers passed quickly at Isvara. His mother often found Nicholas curled up in a comfortable chair in the family's library absorbed in dramatic

Russian tales and legends from long ago. The future archaeologist often thought to himself, "Maybe I can find ancient treasures some day!"

Nicholas did indeed find treasures—and he didn't have to wait long. A well-known archaeologist named L.K. Ivanovsky visited the family at Isvara when Nicholas was about nine. How exciting! And what was even better was that Mr. Ivanovsky invited him to go on an excavation.

"Nicholas, I'm going to start excavating a burial mound near the village today. Would you like to help?" Mr. Ivanovsky asked one day.

"Sure!" Nicholas said. He ran to collect a walking stick and shovel.

Soon the two arrived at the tiny village of Volosovo, which was surrounded by mounds of dirt and jagged stone piles dating back to ancient Russia.

Nicholas helped Mr. Ivanovsky for two days without finding anything but rocks. The third day he was digging, digging, digging through layers of hard-packed dirt. BANG! Nicholas's shovel hit something hard—and it wasn't a rock. Finally he had found something!

"It's a sword! A real sword!" yelled Nicholas, as he uncovered a long metal object.

"Excellent, Nicholas!" called Mr. Ivanovsky. "This is exactly what I was hoping for!"

The sword was the kind that Nicholas's historical heroes had carried. How often he had imagined one just like it in the games he played with his copper-colored wooden sword. This was so much better! Wait until his friends back at school heard about his sword!

Nicholas helped Mr. Ivanovsky whenever he could. Together they found axes, broken pottery, bronze bracelets and even shimmering silver and gold pieces from the tenth and eleventh centuries. Unearthing real relics and treasures just like the ones in his history books made Nicholas's heart pound with excitement.

While he was still a "May bug," Nicholas received permission from the Imperial Archaeological Society to do his own research on the archaeological sites near Isvara. He carefully dug through the layers of dirt to uncover the relics. He kept detailed records of every find and even made sketches showing the exact position of each piece before he moved it. Nicholas developed a lifelong passion for archaeology.

Nicholas was busy with other things too, but he had such concentration that he did everything well. His room overflowed with his collection of artifacts, minerals and plants. He even catalogued birds and collected eggs for the scientific studies of the St. Petersburg Forestry Department.

Nicholas's parents knew that he could finish everything he started, but they could hardly imagine how he kept track of so much. Throughout his life, Nicholas did many things at the same time, without sacrificing quality in anything. That is very hard to do.

Nicholas also developed an interest in hunting, which he came to in an unusual way. Each year when his family returned to the dampness of St. Petersburg, Nicholas caught bronchitis. His doctor had a unique prescription: Nicholas should spend more time outdoors in the winter!

So as a teenager, Nicholas spent long hours trailing various animals in the frigid Russian climate. And it was a frightening experience during a hunting trek that led him to discover his life's work.

CHAPTER 3

A Bear in the Woods

One day fifteen-year-old Nicholas was hunting in the dense forests of his beloved Isvara. His breath formed clouds of steam in the frosty air. Suddenly he stopped and gasped with surprise. An enormous bear was lumbering toward him! The two forest wanderers eyed each other for a long, tense minute. Miraculously, the bear retreated into the lush pines.

But the chance meeting with the bear had a lasting effect on Nicholas. Heart pounding, he ran home. He caught his breath, calmed his nerves and sat down to write about his encounter.

Nicholas's dramatic article was published in a hunting magazine. Nicholas continued to write hunting stories, and he illustrated them with sensitive and detailed sketches.

Nicholas had always loved to draw. He had

drawn landscapes, portraits, sketches of his archaeological finds, and set designs for school performances. But a breakthrough came when a family friend named Mikhail Mikeshin saw Nicholas's work in a hunting magazine.

Mr. Mikeshin was a popular artist. His sculptures are still displayed in Russia today. He also illustrated books, published a journal and painted. On a visit to the Roerich household, Mr. Mikeshin had a chance to talk to Nicholas about his drawings.

"You have never had any drawing lessons?" he asked Nicholas in amazement.

"No," replied Nicholas, "but I want them!" To Nicholas's delight, Mr. Mikeshin offered to become his teacher.

During his lessons Nicholas made an important discovery. "I want to be an artist," he told his parents. Konstantin and Maria were more than a little startled. To them, sketching was just another of the many things that Nicholas did well. There was nothing wrong with art—as a hobby. But this was different.

During the nineteenth century, men often followed their father's profession. Konstantin had expected Nicholas to study law, and he secretly dreamed of the moment when his son would share his practice. Konstantin grumbled about how impractical an artistic career was. "Why shouldn't Nicholas study law and take over my business? Why does he dream of being an artist and cause such an uproar in our household?"

CHAPTER 4

Art Classes and Law Exams

Nicholas was very worried. He wanted to be a good and respectful son. He also wanted to follow his dream. He discussed his problem with his art teacher, who had realized that Nicholas's talent was extraordinary.

"Mr. Mikeshin, I have such a problem. I want so much to be an artist, but my father has his heart set on my studying law!" exclaimed Nicholas. "What can I do?"

Mr. Mikeshin was thoughtful. Then his face brightened. "Nicholas, I have an idea!" he said. "Your father knows that you have always done many things at the same time. Why don't you ask him if you can study at the art academy as well as the university? "

Nicholas pondered this suggestion. Maybe it would work! "I'll try it," he said.

Konstantin agreed to consider his son's unique proposal. Nicholas was only eighteen years old! Yet Konstantin thought he could handle this dual enrollment. Finally he gave his approval. "But you must promise me, Nicholas," he said, "that you will do both things equally well."

It was a challenging compromise. But that was how Nicholas came to study art at the Academy of Arts and law at the Imperial University in St. Petersburg *at the same time*.

Soon the busy student was rushing from painting classes to law exams and back again. Nicholas once commented, "I suppose I'm fated to hurry all my life. I wonder if I'll find time to die."

Nicholas met his best art teacher almost by accident. After completing basic art classes, each student had to choose a specialty and a professor under whom to study until graduation. Nicholas wanted to study historical painting. Although that professor liked Nicholas's work, his historical painting class was already full. So Nicholas had to specialize in landscape painting under Arkhip Kuinji instead.

Mr. Kuinji was once a shepherd boy. His time

alone on the hills watching the clouds passing across the sky profoundly affected his art. His landscapes were meditative, his lighting unusual. He encouraged his students to use simple lines without excessive detail to create a feeling that land, sea and sky were one.

Nicholas still liked historical painting best, but under Mr. Kuinji he learned some important techniques. He learned to create beautiful landscapes in which the sky and the mountains merged.

Mr. Kuinji influenced Nicholas profoundly in many ways. Nicholas later wrote, "I was happy to have as my first teacher an extraordinary man. The eminent Master Kuinji was not only a remarkable artist, but also a great Teacher of life."

Mr. Kuinji recognized his young student's talent, his flair for ancient Russian subjects and his inexhaustible energy. Nicholas made remarkable progress in his studies under Mr. Kuinji, even as he took difficult law exams simultaneously.

One day Mr. Kuinji called Nicholas into his office. Nicholas wondered why his teacher looked so serious.

"Nicholas, I have to talk to you," said Mr.

Kuinji. Nicholas held his breath. Then his teacher's face broke into a wide smile. "I am promoting you to the most advanced art class. This is the second promotion you have earned in a couple of months. This is really extraordinary, Nicholas!" Of course, Nicholas too was overjoyed.

Although he was tired from his schedule, Nicholas also did illustrations for art journals and for a university literary journal. But why would an exhausted student do extra work? He used the money he earned to pay for his art supplies. Since his father was still not in favor of his art studies (even though he supported Nicholas in other ways), Nicholas insisted on paying for his art supplies himself.

Finally it was time for Nicholas to begin his graduation project for the Academy of Arts. He still loved Russian history and spent his spare time in the public library, reading about the lives of Russian saints. As he sat among the dusty history books, wondering what to do as his graduation project, the books gave him an idea.

Nicholas's project was a painting called *The Messenger: Tribe Has Risen against Tribe.* A dejected old man is sitting in a wooden boat being pushed by a man with a pole. This messenger is bringing the devastating news to a neighboring village that the tribes are at war. The scene is primitive, meditative and mysterious—inspired by ancient Russian history. Art critics and students loved it. *The Messenger* was bought for a world-famous art gallery in Moscow. And Nicholas finally earned the coveted title of artist.

NICHOLAS PAINTING AT ISVARA, 1897

CHAPTER 5

Helena: Wife, Friend and Fellow Traveler

After his double graduation in 1897, Nicholas continued to prove that he was a young man who knew what he wanted and stuck with it. Now that he was finished with his schooling, he had time for some social life.

Like many European cities at the turn of the century, St. Petersburg was a thriving cultural center. Nicholas often joined his friends in their salons, gatherings in homes where artists and writers met to discuss current developments in their fields.

Among Nicholas's new friends were Varvara and Alexandra Schneider, sisters who were both artists. He sometimes spent whole days discussing art and literature at the Schneider residence. One popular pastime in this salon was filling out questionnaire books—books with long titles and unusual questions about personal preferences.

One afternoon Varvara pulled Nicholas aside. "Nicholas, look at our new book!" she exclaimed, pointing to a handsomely bound book displayed on a table. Its title was *Confessions: The Album to Record Opinions, Thoughts, Feelings, Ideas, Peculiarities, Impressions, Characteristics of Friends*.

"That is quite a title! What do I do with it?" asked Nicholas.

"You just answer the questions! I think you'll find them intriguing," replied Varvara with a twinkle in her eye.

Nicholas smiled and sat down on the sofa with the book. Soon he started to write, stroking his blond beard as he thought about the questions. The questions were in English, but he wrote his answers in Russian.

Your favorite virtue: indefatigability

Your favorite heroes in real life: Leonardo da Vinci, a monk under the most austere vow

If not yourself, who would you be: a traveler-writer

Your favorite names: Elena, Tatyana, Nina, Ingegerda, Roman, Rostislav, Arseny

Your favorite color: violet, ultramarine, Indian yellow

Nicholas, at age twenty-five, knew himself and his destiny well. Many of his answers proved prophetic.

As early as 1899, Nicholas became a traveler-writer, sent on a trip by the Russian Archaeological Society to study ancient Russian architecture. On his travels he stopped at the estate of a well-known archaeologist named Prince Putyatin.

In the foyer of the house, Nicholas met a charming young woman who would fulfill another *Confessions* book entry. "Who is this?" Nicholas wondered, struck by her grace and beauty. Her thick brunette hair was wound around her head in a shining braid. Expressively arched brows framed her dark, luminous eyes. Her name was Elena Ivanovna Shaposhnikova.

Elena (Helena) was Princess Putyatina's niece. "He looks like a surveyor," she thought, as she led Nicholas into the dining room. Nevertheless, there was a sensitivity in his manner that caught her attention. Over tea, Helena learned that he was an artist.

Nicholas stayed for several days at Prince Putyatin's estate. By then, he was thoroughly enchanted by Helena's beauty and intelligence. She was an excellent pianist and was also interested in art.

Throughout the fall, Nicholas grew more and more fond of Helena. When they were apart, he sometimes wrote to her several times a day. She was five years younger than he but already had several suitors. Nicholas tried to discourage her interest in at least one of them. Obviously, Nicholas was in love. Soon he was writing in his diary, "I am afraid for myself—there are so many good things about her."

As they sat together one afternoon, he took Helena's hand and drew a deep breath.

"Helena," he said nervously. "I cannot imagine being without you. Will you be my wife?"

Helena was also in love. She didn't hesitate. "Yes!" she answered joyfully.

Unfortunately, their wedding had to be postponed because Nicholas's father became ill. After his father's death, Nicholas used his inheritance to go to Paris for a year to study art. He wanted to make the trip a honeymoon, but Nicholas and Helena couldn't afford to go away together for that long. So their marriage was postponed again. When his year in Paris was finished, he hurried home.

On October 28, 1901, Nicholas and Helena were married at the church of the Imperial Academy of the Arts. Thus a lifelong partnership was sealed. Helena was involved in all aspects of Nicholas's vigorous, busy life. She was so humble, though, that she kept out of the public eye. Even when she published her own books, she used pseudonyms.

Nicholas called her "Lada," Russian for "harmony, inspiration and strength." He later dedicated his books to "Elena, my wife, friend, fellow traveler, inspirer!"

Perhaps it was Helena's example of strength and his profound respect for her that later inspired him to write, "Women, indeed you will weave and unfold the Banner of Peace. Fearlessly you will rise up to guard the improvement of Life.... You will pronounce the sacred word Culture."

Women weren't encouraged to do much in Nicholas's day. They were considered mentally inferior, likely to break under the strain of too much intellectual activity. Nicholas took a daring stand in his support of women in the early twentieth century.

CHAPTER 6

The Past: Key to the Future

The chairman of the financial committee of the Society for the Encouragement of the Arts stood up abruptly behind his enormous wooden desk, his chair scraping the floor loudly. He had been interviewing Nicholas for several hours for the position of secretary of the society. Now he looked sharply at Nicholas and said, "And in three days, please show me the annual budget you would put together if you got the job!"

Startled, Nicholas also rose and politely thanked the chairman for the interview. As he left the office, Nicholas felt more than a bit overwhelmed. What a strange test! The chairman had recited a long list of figures, but Nicholas had taken no notes. How could he possibly be expected to put together a budget? But he did have an extraordinary memory—and he needed the job to support his new wife.

Three days later, Nicholas submitted his sample budget. He was competing with older, more experienced applicants. But Nicholas got the job! The other applicants were extremely annoyed to be beaten by a twenty-six-year-old youngster. Nicholas and Helena, of course, were relieved and happy.

In 1906, Nicholas was named director of the school run by the Society for the Encouragement of the Arts, in spite of those who opposed his appointment. He and his family, which now included four-year-old George and two-year-old Svetoslav, moved into the school building. He quickly changed the curriculum of the school, adding many new classes such as ceramics, glass painting and even singing.

Nicholas hired new staff and began holding regular faculty meetings to discuss his proposals for the school. Faculty meetings were an innovative idea at the time. He was personally involved with the students, even taking them on field trips to old Russian cities to teach them about art and architecture. The school grew to include two thousand students of all social classes. Its annual art exhibition attracted the attention of everyone in St. Petersburg.

Even though Nicholas was busy, he found time to paint and to study archaeology. He painted many rustic scenes with enormous skies and tiny people, to show how small and subservient man is relative to Mother Nature.

During this period, Nicholas did a collection of seventy-five paintings of old churches, heavy stone towers, lonely monasteries and romantic castles. His subjects often dated back to the twelfth century. Nicholas once wrote, "A man who does not understand the past cannot think of the future." His goal was to make people aware of their cultural heritage so they would want to preserve the beauty of the past.

Some of Nicholas's paintings were later sent to a Russian exhibit in St. Louis, Missouri. Nicholas said, with great hope, "Let these paintings be my benevolent messengers to America." Remember these messengers! America was an important part of Nicholas's destiny.

And now Nicholas began a new kind of work that was to make him famous in the West.

CHAPTER 7

Bravo for Backdrops!

Paris, May 19, 1909. Opening night of *Prince Igor (Scenes and Polovtsian Dances)*. Costumes and set design by Nicholas Roerich.

A band of barbarians leaps and dances in a frenzy against a brilliant red and gold backdrop. With quick strokes of their shiny sabers they slice the air. They rush toward the audience in a thrilling display of strength.

"Bravo! Bravo!" the crowd shouts. People climb on the velvet seats. They scream. They weep. They wave handkerchiefs. Then something completely unprecedented happens. The audience rushes forward, tears down the orchestra rail and grabs the performers to hug them!

It would be an understatement to say that Nicholas's costumes and backdrops were a fantastic success. But why did Nicholas add yet another activity to his overloaded schedule? Probably because he enjoyed it so much. It was a perfect blend of art forms for him.

Some of Nicholas's best work was for a play called *Peer Gynt*. Peer is a lying, mischievous scamp who leaves his widowed mother to seek his fortune. Nicholas used brilliant colors for the sets depicting Peer's tempestuous young years, such as violets, vivid greens, bright blues and oranges.

Peer has many disastrous adventures. He falls in love with a young girl, but he leaves her, too. He finds wealth and success in life, but not happiness. The colors Nicholas chose for the later sets were more subdued, perfectly befitting the older, sadder man. Peer eventually returns home to marry his sweetheart, who has remained faithful to him. Nicholas's final set showed a small hut in the mountains, symbolizing their humble contentment.

It was almost opening night of *Peer Gynt*, and Nicholas was checking every detail. He wanted the sets to have the texture of the natural objects they represented, and the costumes to look well-worn.

"You must be more careful with the colors," he said to the artists working on the sets. "Look at the blue of the clouds in the sketch! It is much fresher and purer than the color you are using.

"And the lighting isn't right. I want some violet lamps at the top of the mill, and some orange ones, too," he said. "You will see how much better it looks." The set artists began at once to make the changes he requested.

Then Nicholas turned his attention to the costumes. "This shawl looks too new," said Nicholas to an assistant. "Why don't you try tearing it? And the whole costume looks much too clean. Dip it in black coffee. That will surely give it a used look and an earthy tone."

"Coffee?" exclaimed the startled assistant. But he took the costume and went off to work on it. The next day the costume looked much more realistic.

The critics didn't like the play *Peer Gynt*, but they loved Nicholas's sets and costumes. One critic wrote, "The whole production was a celebration of his brush."

Meanwhile, back at Nicholas's office, things went on at their usual frantic pace. "Professor Roerich, here are your papers to sign," his secretary said, placing a stack of documents on Nicholas's desk. A guest was already in the office, discussing plans with Nicholas as he painted.

"Thank you," said Nicholas to the secretary, as he reached for the ringing telephone, paintbrush still in hand. After the phone call, he signed the papers.

"Sir, you have another visitor," a servant breathlessly announced, running into the room. And off Nicholas dashed, wiping paint from his hands and calling to his first guest to stay for lunch. The afternoon was packed with meetings and more telephone calls, as Nicholas continued to work on canvases and set designs.

Nicholas probably owed his great success as a set designer to the many hours he spent studying the music and the drama. "I study both deeply," he wrote, "in order to get at the spirit that lies behind both. I then endeavor to express the same thought, the same inspiration in my painting, that the composer and the librettist have expressed in music and in words."

Through his set designs, Nicholas's influence was extending to an ever-widening circle in the artistic world.

CHAPTER 8

Nicholas in America

"Professor Roerich, you are not at all well. Have you been overexerting yourself again?" asked the doctor, as he gazed at the artist sternly.

"I do feel terrible," Nicholas sighed. "What is wrong with me?"

"You have pneumonia, and you must get out of the city," the doctor said. "And please, Professor, do slow down! You do the work of ten men, yet you are never satisfied. Any other man would drop dead from so much work!"

Nicholas was forced to agree with the doctor. The Roerichs moved across the border to Finland in 1916 to get out of the city. In spite of his poor health, Nicholas continued painting. He also became more interested in Eastern philosophy and began planning a trip to India.

By 1918 Nicholas was well enough to begin

raising money for the trip. The family went to England so Nicholas could do some set designs, exhibit his work and get visas.

But one day he came into the living room and greeted his wife sadly. "Helena, it's final. They can't pay me for my set designs. We have to cancel our trip to India."

"I know you are disappointed—so am I! But things will work out," replied Helena sympathetically.

Helena was, as always, his support and hope. More importantly, she was right. As that door of opportunity closed, another opened: the director of the Art Institute of Chicago invited Nicholas to exhibit his work there. Nicholas, Helena and their two sons sailed to America in September 1920. Several hundred paintings went with them.

Nicholas's first exhibit was in December at the Kingore Gallery in New York City. There had never been such a large exhibit by a Russian artist in America.

Nicholas's paintings caused quite a stir. No one had ever seen such colors! "Oooohs" and "aaaahs" echoed through the halls. The catalogue for the exhibit at the Kingore Gallery described Nicholas's colors as "magical in their depth and subtlety." Some of his paintings were sold to the owners of New York's best collections.

Nicholas and his canvases traveled to twenty-eight American cities over the next year and a half. Nicholas loved America and the energy and enthusiasm he found everywhere.

Nicholas also loved the land, especially the rocky, windy coasts of Maine. The golden-hued, rugged majesty of the Grand Canyon inspired him, and he was enthusiastic about meeting some Native Americans. But even when he was enjoying himself, his intense pace worried Helena.

"Nicholas, remember what the doctor said," admonished Helena. "You must slow down!"

Nicholas knew Helena was right. His days, as usual, were packed with activity from morning until night. A normal day for Nicholas would exhaust anyone else.

"But what can I give up?" asked Nicholas. "I love giving lectures at museums and universities—these Americans need to learn more about art. I must see my guests, and I must paint for several hours each day. Then there are our future trips to plan. What can I leave undone?"

In America Nicholas's expansive nature inspired him to found two international art organizations and a school. The credo of the school began, "Art will unify all humanity. Art is one—indivisible. Art has its many branches, yet all are one. Art is the manifestation of the coming synthesis. Art is for all."

Nicholas also introduced Americans to new ideas in other ways. He gave a revolutionary lecture on the "spiritual garment" at Marshall Field's department store in Chicago.

"Humanity does not understand how important the aura is. In fact, clothing can be harmonized to the human aura," Nicholas said to the shoppers. People glanced at each other with raised eyebrows.

"How can that be done?" asked a bold lady, who managed to find her voice despite her shock at Nicholas's strange topic.

"Color has mystic power," replied Nicholas. "People have made such drab flowers of themselves! Color can help create a worshipful atmosphere in a church, or promote healing in a hospital. We could find power and joy if we used color the way they did in the Italian Renaissance!"

"I see—or rather, I think I see," said the woman doubtfully, as she looked down at her tan skirt and brown shoes. "Thank you, Professor. Maybe I will buy some more colorful clothes today at Marshall's!" The crowd chuckled.

A final achievement in America was the founding of the Nicholas Roerich Museum in November 1923. Eventually, a twenty-four-story building was built to display his work and house his school and international art center. Nicholas's paintings were hung on the first three floors. Thousands of people from all over the world gathered for the building's grand opening to pay tribute to Nicholas.

In 1923, Nicholas was on the verge of fulfilling a lifelong desire: he was going to Asia!

CHAPTER 9

Kanchenjunga at Last

Nicholas, Helena and their grown sons sailed for India on November 17, 1923. Their Asian expedition was to take almost five years and cover 15,500 miles.

Although Svetoslav soon returned to America, George stayed with his parents for the entire trip. This was a special help to them because he was an expert on Oriental languages and acted as their translator.

The Roerichs visited many cultural sites, then settled near Darjeeling for more than a year to complete the plans for their expedition. From their window, they enjoyed a view of a particularly magnificent mountain.

"Helena, I know that mountain!" exclaimed Nicholas.

"Really? What mountain is it?" asked Helena.

"Remember that painting at Isvara that I told you about?" Nicholas replied. "This is the same mountain—Kanchenjunga. It's a sacred spot. Hermits still live in caves behind this mountain. I used to stare at the painting when I was a boy, and imagine all the adventures I would have when I grew up. And here I am at last!"

The Roerichs planned their journey carefully. Their route circled Central Asia, passing through what is now India, Tibet, Pakistan, China, Russia and Mongolia. Such a trip had never been completed by Westerners before. It was so dangerous that even seasoned explorers avoided certain spots.

But Nicholas wasn't thinking about danger—he was thinking about art! He later wrote, "As an artist my main aspiration in Asia was toward artistic work, and it is difficult to say how soon I shall record all my artistic impressions and paint from my sketches—so generous are these gifts of Asia."

The group left Darjeeling in March 1925. They went first to Srinagar in the western Himalayas to prepare their gear. This was no small effort in itself, since they had to be entirely self-sufficient for their journey.

In August they set off along an ancient caravan route toward a city called Leh. The group included nine Europeans, thirty-six native guides and porters, and 102 camels, yaks, mules and horses.

One night they set up camp at a village near Leh where the elevation was 11,000 feet. Helena went into their tent, where Nicholas was already asleep. As she touched a woolen blanket on the bed, a pinkish-violet flame almost a foot high shot up. She cried, "Fire! Fire!" Nicholas was instantly awake.

"What is it?" he said. Helena tried to put out the flame with her hands. It burst through her fingers and became a group of smaller flames.

"How amazing!" said Nicholas. "It must be some sort of an electrical phenomenon."

"Yes, it's not hot like a real fire, just warm." Helena showed him her palms. "My hands are not burned, and neither is the blanket. Look! Now the flame is completely gone!"

They talked about the extraordinary flame until they fell asleep. They were to have other experiences of amazing electrical phenomena at very high altitudes.

The expedition spent almost a month in Leh. It

was a typical Tibetan town, with clay walls, spectacular temples and stupas, and mountains all around. The Roerichs saw loud caravans and bustling bazaars. And they also heard fascinating legends of Jesus' travels in the East.

A Buddhist monk told Nicholas these extraordinary stories. Jesus, whom they called Issa, had come to India with a merchant's caravan to study in the Himalayas. The monk pointed out a tree near a pond where Jesus preached to the people before he went to Palestine. Buddhist legends said that Jesus was rescued from the cross by his disciples and later taught in Srinagar. He was buried in a tomb marked, "Here lies the son of Joseph."

Nicholas was fascinated. He tried to find out more about the legends of St. Issa in a famous monastery at Himis. The lamas initially denied everything. But bit by bit, the stories came out. The lamas finally showed Nicholas manuscripts about St. Issa, lying in dark corners—maybe chewed on by Tibetan mice!

Nicholas was much inspired by these legends. He wrote, "From this site of the sermons of Issa, from its high terraces, one must paint a series of all that can be seen from here. In these high places, purified by winds, occurred the signs of great communions."

Another source of inspiration was the people. Women especially were colorfully dressed. They wore tall fur caps with earpieces turned up. Their jewelry, made from bright turquoise and shiny metal, hung down their backs. They each wore the skin of a yak across their shoulders.

The women were always gracious to the travelers. They ran up to the Roerichs as they were leaving the city.

"We want to wish you a safe journey!" they cried. "Please allow us to sprinkle this yak's milk on your foreheads. It has been blessed—it will protect you!"

Nicholas thanked them and the women gave everyone in their group the blessing—even the animals!

It turned out that the blessing was sorely needed. The Roerichs had to go over seven icy mountain passes so cold that they had to wear fur boots, fur caps and even fur socks. At one point George was riding across a slick glacier and almost fell off his horse into a deep abyss.

The party went north to China, to a place called Khotan. Two Chinese officials stopped them and demanded to see their passports.

"These papers are not valid," one of them declared.

"But these visas are from your embassy in Paris," protested Nicholas.

"They are not valid!" barked the official. "You must remain here. You must give us your weapons. You may not do any research here, and you may not sketch anything outdoors. We cannot allow you to draw topographical maps of this area!"

"Maps?" exclaimed Nicholas in surprise. "I am an artist. I do not draw maps!"

"Those are our orders," snapped the second man. "You may paint, but only inside."

Nicholas and his friends had no choice. They were forced to spend four months in Khotan in the winter, without adequate supplies. Most of their animals and several people in their group died, but the Roerich family was spared.

Nicholas did seven beautiful paintings in Khotan, in spite of the obstacles. One painting,

NICHOLAS HOLDING THE TANKA OF SHAMBALLA IN MONGOLIA, 1927

called *The Banner of the Coming One*, illustrates a scene in the western Himalayas. A group of people are looking at a tanka, or banner, of Shamballa. A lama in a red robe and a yellow cap is pointing at the tanka with a stick and explaining something. And guess who is in the middle of the tanka? The legendary ruler of Shamballa, Rigden Djapo, whom Nicholas well remembered from the midnight tales he had heard as a child in St. Petersburg. A fierce battle against darkness is depicted below him.

The Roerichs' journey continued over the Altai Mountains until they reached a place where the legends of Shamballa were everywhere: Mongolia. The Mongols, with their colorful clothes and tall cone-shaped red hats, came to visit the Roerichs' camp on horseback. They noticed the banner of Shamballa that flew over the camp, and the American flag tied to a Mongolian spear. When they saw Nicholas's pictures of the skyscrapers of New York, they exclaimed with sincere delight, "The land of Shamballa!"

Nicholas enjoyed the Mongols. He subscribed to the theory that the Native Americans had migrated to America from Siberia. He was intrigued by the similarities in the features, customs, dress and songs of the Native Americans and the Mongols.

Nicholas discovered an ancient Mongolian legend about two brothers who were neighbors. A fiery dragon stirred and split the earth. The split came between the lands of the two brothers and separated them. The brothers missed each other, and they asked the birds to carry messages back and forth. The legend says that the two brothers are waiting for a heavenly bird to carry them over the gap and reunite them.

When Nicholas showed the Mongols photographs of Native Americans they exclaimed, "But those are Mongols!" Nicholas felt this was because the "separated brothers" recognized each other.

The Roerichs had many more adventures on their way across the Gobi Desert and the Tibetan plateau. Their journey ended on May 26, 1928, when they finally returned to Darjeeling. In spite of cruel and uncooperative officials, dangerous mountain passes and bitter weather, Nicholas did about five hundred paintings on their trek. His travels also gave him material for many books.

Nicholas was the first artist to bring the beauty of the Himalayas to the West. As he viewed the snowy peaks, he wrote, "The highest knowledge, the most inspired songs, the most superb sounds and colors are created on the mountains. . . . The high mountains stand as witnesses of the great reality." And no one has ever painted those mountains as well as Nicholas Roerich.

CHAPTER 10

Wow, What Colors!

Soviet cosmonaut Yuri Gagarin was the first man to orbit the earth. In April 1961 he described what he saw from space: "Rays were blazing through the atmosphere of the earth, the horizon became bright orange, gradually passing into all the colors of the rainbow: from light blue to dark blue, to violet and then to black. What an indescribable gamut of colors! Just like the paintings of the artist Nicholas Roerich."

Gagarin was right—the colors Nicholas used are truly out of this world! In addition to mountains, Nicholas's use of color became one of his trademarks. In the *Confessions* book Nicholas signed when he was just twenty-five, he had listed his favorite colors as violet, ultramarine and Indian yellow. He often used these colors in his paintings.

Nicholas's colors have been described like this:

"His blue is the blue of the northern twilight; his green is the green of the sea-grass; his red is the red of the beacon fires, and his flame—is from Byzantine arrows." Nicholas even wrote poems that described what these colors meant to him. He thought colors had symbolic mystical power: blue stands for peace, green for wisdom and red for courage.

Nicholas used unusual shades and colors that no one else used. He once wrote, "Just as a composer when writing the score chooses a certain key to write in, so I paint in a certain key, a key of color."

How did Nicholas make his paintings so vivid and the colors so clear? He used tempera because the colors are fresh and long-lasting. First he put down a layer of a single color—perhaps ultramarine, emerald green, crimson or sapphire blue. After this ground layer dried, he quickly painted over it to finish the work. Because the original layer was so dazzling, the finished painting was extraordinary.

Throughout his life, Nicholas enjoyed discussing art with his family in their evenings together. One night at their family home, Svetoslav, who was by then a well-known artist himself, brought in a journal article to show Nicholas.

"Father, you really must read this. An art teacher is actually telling his students not to be concerned about whether the colors of their paints will last!"

Helena smiled. "That sounds odd. It's a bit like suggesting to a writer that it's all right to use disappearing ink."

Nicholas took a sip of steaming tea. "What an unfortunate attitude to pass on to the next generation of artists," he said. "Better to learn the lessons of time from the paintings of long ago that have darkened or faded."

"What causes that darkening, Father?" asked George.

"Poor-quality oil paints, for one," replied Nicholas. "They decompose. Then too, different shades of paint sometimes have incompatible ingredients that react over time to produce muddy colors. And some artists layered on so much fixative to make the paint dry that their paintings later took on a dingy look."

"But in some cases the old masters knew more than we do about making good materials," added Svetoslav. "I wish we knew how the Italian masters made the drying oils that they used to preserve their paintings."

"Yes," agreed Nicholas, "but we probably never will. That was a closely guarded secret. All we know is that the oil was kept in monasteries in earthen pots for years and years before use. Each master had his own special container of the oil."

"I'd love to have some to use on the painting of Mother that I'm working on," said Svetoslav with a

HELENA ROERICH, PASSPORT PHOTO, 1919

loving glance in Helena's direction. "My oils are not so bright as the tempera you use, Father, but I still want them to last. And I want Mother to always look as beautiful in the painting as she does in real life today."

"You have used good materials, Svetoslav," said Nicholas. "I am sure that your portrait will be a fitting tribute to your mother's beauty for many years to come."

Nicholas studied the styles and techniques of the old masters, but he never fit into any single artistic tradition. Edgar Lansbury, president of the Nicholas Roerich Museum, once wrote: "Roerich defies categorizing. He is a man who created his own style."

Although some people find it hard to believe, Nicholas created about seven thousand paintings in his lifetime. He was truly a transcendent artist. And through his magnificent colors and unique style, he conveyed a glimpse of heaven and a sense of his own deep spirituality.

CHAPTER 11

Dreams and Prophecies

Nicholas was a profoundly spiritual person. Unlike most other painters, he painted to remind the souls of his viewers of spiritual worlds beyond earth. His inner life made Nicholas a great man.

Nicholas's spirituality began during his childhood. As a young boy, he had a certain recurring dream.

"Mama!" Nicholas would call. "Mama, I had that dream again." And Nicholas's mother would come running into his bedroom.

"Tell me about it," she would say.

"It was the same as always," Nicholas would reply. "This figure was close to me, so close I could feel clothes swishing against me! I couldn't see the face. The robes weren't like any I have seen. They were white! The figure seemed very serious. Is this supposed to tell me something about heaven?"

"I don't know, dear," his mother would say. "Go back to sleep now." And Nicholas would go back to sleep.

He was profoundly affected by these dreams. Perhaps they helped orient him toward spiritual realms and toward the connectedness of all religions.

Later, Nicholas and Helena didn't believe in just one religion. They were interested in many Eastern beliefs. Their philosophy combined Hinduism, Buddhism, Theosophy and agni yoga.

The Theosophical Society was founded in 1875 by Helena P. Blavatsky. She communed with Eastern spiritual teachers (gurus), especially with the Master M. and the Master K.H., and she became their student (chela). The beliefs of Theosophy included karma, reincarnation and the special relationship between the guru and the chela.

The guru-chela relationship was a theme in many of Nicholas's paintings. In *Pearl of Searching*, the guru is looking thoughtfully at a pearl necklace with his chela. This symbolizes the "pearl of great price" that gives purpose to life. The people are in the lower foreground, with clouds in the middle and mountains in the distance. This basic theme and layout is found in many of Nicholas's paintings.

Nicholas and Helena believed that service to others was the best way to show devotion to God. They especially loved the Indian saint Ramakrishna.

Many of Nicholas's paintings show saints and great teachers doing good works. One such painting is *St. Panteleimon—The Healer*. St. Panteleimon was a gentle healer who was an expert on herbs. His name means "All-Merciful." Nicholas's painting shows the saint doing a most practical job: gathering herbs from a field of colorful flowers.

St. Panteleimon withstood many trials because he refused to renounce his faith. On the emperor's orders, he was placed in kettle of tar. Miraculously, the tar remained cool. He was tied to a boulder and thrown into the sea, but the boulder became light and he floated on the water. This saint survived everything.

Another common theme in Nicholas's work is spiritual fire. This concept comes from the ancient teaching of agni yoga, the science of achieving union with God through the sacred fire.

The idea that fire would come out of the mountain to enlighten humanity is illustrated in Nicholas's painting *Burning of Darkness*. Three mysterious figures are coming out of a dark blue mountain. One carries a glowing chest representing the sacred fire. As Nicholas explains in the book *Agni Yoga*, "All actions must be infused by the purifying fiery striving." In 1920 Nicholas and Helena formed groups to study agni yoga. The Agni Yoga Society continues to publish their books.

Some amazingly prophetic paintings grew out of Nicholas's spiritual life. For instance, he did several paintings between 1912 and 1914 that seem to portend danger for Russia. *Cry of the Serpent*, painted in 1913, depicts a huge red serpent in front of a barren landscape, raising its head in a shriek.

Years later, Nicholas learned of the ancient Eastern legend that when a serpent cries, it is a warning that the country is in danger of destruction. Perhaps Nicholas was somehow aware of the coming Bolshevik Revolution of 1917, which he did not support—the revolution that was to cause so much trauma in his native land.

Nicholas himself lived two prophecies. When he was a small child, a priest predicted that Nicholas would have an illness when he was seven. Nicholas did indeed get sick at that age.

The priest had also told Nicholas, "You must not be ailing—you will have to work hard for the sake of Russia." Nicholas did get well, and he did work hard all his life. The only inaccuracy in the priest's prophecy was that Nicholas's work was not just for the sake of Russia. It was for the sake of the whole world!

CHAPTER 12

Three Dots in a Circle

Nicholas didn't have any small ideas—only big ones. One of his biggest ideas was about how to protect art objects during times of war. Nicholas had a simple idea: to create a special banner to be flown over museums, cathedrals, libraries and universities during wartime. He wanted all nations to sign a treaty agreeing to honor the banner and not destroy buildings that flew it, even if the nations became enemies.

Nicholas designed the banner and promoted the treaty, which many nations signed. The treaty became known as the Roerich Pact, and the banner is called the Banner of Peace.

The Banner of Peace is white. In the center are three red dots surrounded by a red ring. How did Nicholas come up with this symbol? Here is a hint: he often looked to the past. This symbol is in the

Temple of Heaven in Beijing. It is on the images of the ruler of Shamballa, Rigden Djapo. In Mongolia, it was even branded on horses.

Riding in Mongolia one day, Nicholas and Helena passed a rocky outcropping. Bending close, Nicholas saw three dots enclosed by a circle.

"This symbol is so widespread," he remarked to Helena. "I have seen it on Russian icons, Ethiopian antiquities and Neolithic pottery. Do you know what this could be? This is the perfect symbol for the Banner of Peace!"

"That is a wonderful idea—it is familiar to so many people all over the world," Helena agreed. "Such a beautiful symbol."

Nicholas mused about it as they rode on. "Three dots. One could stand for art, one for science and one for religion. The circle could be the circle of culture surrounding all. Or it could be seen as the past, present and future achievements of humanity guarded within the circle of eternity. Either way, this symbol will be meaningful to people everywhere."

Nicholas used this symbol in some of his paintings, such as *Madonna Oriflamma*, which was to represent the Peace Pact. A purple-robed madonna holds up the Banner of Peace.

In another painting, *St. Sophia—The Almighty's Wisdom*, a horseman carries the banner across a fiery orange sky. Underneath the rider is a city surrounded by a wall, symbolizing how the Banner of Peace will protect culture wherever it flies.

Nicholas was nominated for the Nobel Peace Prize because of his efforts to protect the world's culture. The nominating committee said, "The works of Roerich have, for the last thirty years, been one of the great summons to the world for love among men."

The Roerich Pact was promoted through international conferences in cities all over the world. Many famous people were in favor of it, including Albert Einstein. President Roosevelt and representatives of twenty-one countries signed the Roerich Pact in the White House on April 15, 1935. This was a high point of Nicholas's fame in America.

Today, the Banner of Peace is the symbol for the Nicholas Roerich Museum in New York. The museum's motto is *"Pax cultura"*—"Peace through culture." Promoters of the Roerich Pact are encouraging still more nations to sign it.

After his Asian expedition ended in 1928, Nicholas's love of the awe-inspiring Himalayas prompted him to look for a home in India. He and Helena moved to a two-story house in the Kulu Valley in the foothills of the western Himalayas. There he spent the rest of his life.

CHAPTER 13

The Eagle Takes Flight

At Kulu, Nicholas happily painted the dazzling mountains all around him. The ever-changing lavenders, pinks and purples inspired him. He loved the fragrant forests full of cedar, pine, maple and birch trees, and the colorful wildflowers in spring. He explored the entire place on foot and horseback.

Nicholas kept up his rigorous schedule and his good humor. His secretary wrote that Nicholas was never "idle, inactive, scattered or fussy." Nicholas had a regular routine because he never wanted to waste time. He got up early each day and ate breakfast. Then he dictated an article or several letters. He took a walk, typically making sketches on pieces of wood or cardboard, which he stuffed into his backpack. He painted at least until lunchtime. And as always, the family gathered in the evening to talk about their day's work or listen to music.

Once a fellow artist complained to Nicholas, "My studio is so small and dark, like yours. Don't you find it difficult to work at three or four easels in such a tiny space?"

Nicholas replied with a smile, "The cell of Fra Angelico sufficed for *him* to paint!"

Nicholas's appearance had changed a little. His beard was totally white. He usually wore a round

NICHOLAS IN HIS KULU STUDIO

cap and a flowing black wool cape. A friend described him as follows: "Tall, gray-bearded and benign, he resembles a grand old patriarch, but equally a beautiful, loving 'Little Grandfather,' as the Russians would say."

Near his home, Nicholas started a research institute called Urusvati, which means "light of the morning star" in Sanskrit. The institute studied the many things the Roerichs had discovered on their Himalayan expedition, such as different types of plants and Asian art and archaeology. But when World War II started, all scientific work stopped.

Nicholas was horrified by what the war did to his beloved Russia. He pleaded with his friends in America for assistance and founded the American-Russian Cultural Association to help his homeland. One of his last desires was to return to Russia, but unfortunately, this desire was never fulfilled.

In July of 1947, his heart condition worsened and he had surgery. But by December he was at his easel again. Helena came into the studio on a December morning.

"Nicholas, remember what the doctors said. You must be careful," she cautioned. But as she glanced at the beautiful canvas he was working on, she understood why he wanted to keep on painting.

"It's just beautiful, Nicholas," she said softly. They studied the canvas together. A white eagle is gliding toward a chela, who is sitting on a mountaintop in the lotus position. "Are you ever sad to part with your paintings, Nicholas?"

"Oh no," Nicholas replied. "After I finish a painting, I have no feeling of possession—it should go on traveling."

Nicholas named his last painting *The Master's Command*. It was a symbolic painting of the end of his life.

Nicholas Roerich's soul took flight on December 13, 1947. Although his physical heart had failed, his mission was accomplished. He had succeeded in promoting worldwide cultural unity through his art, writings and scientific achievements. Best of all, everyone who sees his paintings is reminded of spiritual realms.

Nicholas had fulfilled the dreams of his childhood. For all his days on earth and in his many professions, Nicholas Roerich was an overcomer, rich in glory—truly a warrior of light.

Select Bibliography

Decter, Jacqueline, with the Nicholas Roerich Museum. *Nicholas Roerich: The Life and Art of a Russian Master.* Rochester, Vt.: Park Street Press, 1989.

Fosdick, Sina. *Nicholas Roerich.* New York: Nicholas Roerich Museum, 1964.

Meador, Shirley. "Nicholas Roerich: Heroes, Myths, and Ageless Mountains." American Artist Magazine 38 (1974).

Nicholas Roerich Museum. *Nicholas Roerich.* New York: Nicholas Roerich Museum, 1974.

Paelian, Garabed. *Nicholas Roerich.* Agoura, Calif.: Aquarian Educational Group, 1974.

Prophet, Elizabeth Clare. *The Lost Years of Jesus.* Corwin Springs, Mont.: Summit University Press, 1987.

Roerich, Nicholas. *Agni Yoga.* New York: Agni Yoga Society, 1980.

———. *Heart of Asia.* Rochester, Vt.: Inner Traditions International, 1990.

———. *The Invincible.* New York: Nicholas Roerich Museum, 1974.

———. *Shambhala.* New York: Nicholas Roerich Museum, 1978.

The Roerich Pact and Banner of Peace. New York: The Roerich Pact and Banner of Peace Committee, 1947.

Acknowledgments

This book would not have happened without the enthusiastic support of Daniel Entin, director of the Nicholas Roerich Museum, who selflessly carries on Nicholas Roerich's work. Words cannot convey my gratitude for his gracious permission to use the cover painting, the photographs and the quotations from the works of Nicholas and Helena Roerich.

A pilgrimage to the Nicholas Roerich Museum is essential for those who wish to experience the true mystical messages of Roerich's paintings. The museum is located at 319 West 107th Street in New York City. Its web site is www.roerich.org.

Jacqueline Decter's meticulous work in *Nicholas Roerich: The Life and Art of a Russian Master* was invaluable in the preparation of this book.

I am especially indebted to Norman Millman and Nigel Yorwerth of Summit University Press for their support and to Nancy Hearn for her vision and her mastery in so many areas of publishing. No writer could ask for a more thorough and sensitive editor than Catherine Bielitz, who polished the manuscript in her gracious and joyful way. Many thanks also to James Bennett for his fantastic cover design, which conveys the spirit of Roerich so well.

And last, my gratitude to my husband, Perry, and to my children, Michael and Tiffany, for their constant encouragement.

The books in the Masters of Life series
are inspirational biographies of heroes from
all spiritual traditions. Their creativity, courage
and dedication to principles made them revolu-
tionaries in their fields. They took the highest road
and became masters of their destiny.